FULL-COLOR UNIFORMS

of the

PRUSSIAN ARMY

72 Plates from the Year 1830

L. SACHSE & Co.

Dover Publications, Inc.
New York

Published in Canada by General Publishing Company, Ltd., 30 Lesmill Road, Don Mills, Toronto, Ontario.
Published in the United Kingdom by Constable and Company, Ltd., 10 Orange Street, London WC2H 7EG.

This Dover edition, first published in 1981, contains all 72 plates from the original portfolio *Das preussische Heer* (full title given in Publisher's Note), first published by L. Sachse & Co., Berlin, in 1830.
The Publisher's Note was written, and the picture captions translated (as a List of Plates), specially for the present edition by Stanley Appelbaum.

International Standard Book Number: 0-486-24085-1
Library of Congress Catalog Card Number: 80-69161

Manufactured in the United States of America
Dover Publications, Inc.
180 Varick Street
New York, N.Y. 10014

List of Plates

Publisher's Note

Many interesting strands of both artistic and military history come together in the magnificent lithographic portfolio of 1830 reproduced here. In the eighteenth and nineteenth centuries, all aspects of life in Prussia, including the periods of prosperity that allowed the arts to flourish, appeared to be closely linked to the nation's military effectiveness. The Hohenzollern rulers, strong personalities all, influenced public activities to a large extent, and Friedrich Wilhelm III, reigning monarch in 1830, was essentially a military man—a rather dry and dour cavalry officer—with a strong interest in beautifying Berlin.

The powerful military machine created by Prussian king Friedrich Wilhelm I (reigned 1713–1740) and further improved by his famous son Frederick the Great (Friedrich II, 1740–1786), was allowed to decay by Frederick the Great's nephew and successor, the reckless profligate Friedrich Wilhelm II (1786–1797). This situation left Prussia an easy prey for the ambitious Napoleon, who conquered and humiliated the nation (campaigns of 1806–1807). Political reforms, a salutary wave of patriotism and above all a thorough reorganization of the Prussian army by Scharnhorst and others, made the "wars of liberation" of 1813–1815 highly successful, and the Prussian general Blücher helped to vanquish Napoleon. Prussia emerged from the ensuing peace conference, the Congress of Vienna, as a major European power, vastly increased in area and prestige. Later on in the reign of Friedrich Wilhelm III (1797–1840), the Customs Union made Prussia the economic leader of the (still not unified) German states.

In the peaceful 1820s and 1830s, Berlin was a major center of the arts. Splendid Neoclassical and Greek Revival public buildings and monuments, such as the Altes Museum, were erected, and important painters and sculptors lived and worked there. A major breakthrough in the lively print market was the introduction of lithography. Invented by Alois Senefelder in Munich in the 1790s, lithography quickly became an important method of commercial reproduction, and before very long was discovered by artists as a fine-art medium capable of quite different effects from engravings and etchings. Hundreds of lithographs were produced in Berlin before 1820, but it was not until after that date that the most famous and long-lasting litho printshops were established.

One of the two or three leading printers was Louis Friedrich Sachse (1798–1877), who set up his Lithographic Institute in his native Berlin in 1828, after long training in his profession. In 1821 he had been a draftsman at the Prussian Royal Lithographic Institute (connected with the Ministry of War for cartographic purposes from 1818, used for art lithography from 1821); then he had studied six years in Paris, where the art was making especially rapid progress, and finally for a brief period with Senefelder himself. Sachse's chief success in Berlin was with portrait lithography, a genre that had been popularized by the well-liked local artist and bon vivant Franz Krüger, but the shop also produced topographical views of towns and landscapes, traditional genre scenes, animal plates, witty cartoons about everyday life in Berlin, and a miscellany of other types. Adolph Menzel, who was to become the single most brilliant artist of nineteenth-century Berlin, worked for Sachse in his youth and produced his own earliest fine-art lithos in the shop. In 1839 Sachse purchased daguerreotype equipment in Paris and became one of the earliest commercial photographers in Germany. By the 1850s photography had largely supplanted lithography as the medium for making inexpensive portraits, and Sachse became principally a picture dealer and exhibitor, handling the work of many of the very greatest German painters of the time. Between 1828 and 1858 his shop had produced about 1500 lithographs; the firm was not totally dissolved until 1876.

One of Sachse's monumental productions was the 72-plate series of hand-colored lithographs reproduced here in its entirety. The original title on the wrappers reads in translation: "The Prussian Army. Published and most humbly dedicated to His Majesty King Frederick William III of Prussia by the art firm of L. Sachse & Co. Drawn and lithographed by L. Elzholz [sic], C. Rechlin, J. Schulz. Printed in the publisher's Lithographic Institute, Berlin, 1830." Of the three contributing artists, two were natives of Berlin and had studied at the Royal Academy there: Ludwig Elsholtz and Carl Rechlin. Elsholtz (1805–1850) became famous for his paintings about the 1813–1815 "wars of liberation" and received numerous royal commissions. Rechlin (ca. 1804–1882) also became a painter of military subjects. "J. Schulz" was probably Johann Karl Schulz (1801–1873) of Danzig, a muralist and printmaker who was active in Berlin from 1828 to

DAS PREUSSISCHE HEER

herausgegeben und

Sr. Majestät dem Könige

Friedrich Wilhelm III von Preussen

allerunterthänigst gewidmet

von

der **KUNSTHANDLUNG** von

L. SACHSE & C?

Gezeichnet und lithographirt

L. Elzholz. C. Rechlin. J. Schulz.

von

Gedruckt im lithographischen Institut

der Herausgeber

BERLIN

1830.

[Title of original wrappers]

1832 before returning home to head the Danzig art school. (Another possibility is Julius Carl Schulz, a painter of military and hunting subjects who exhibited in Berlin between 1824 and 1846.) Elsholtz and Rechlin (and Johann Karl Schulz, if he is the right one) were quite young at the time of the *Prussian Army* project, possibly still students; it has been very common in the history of art for youngsters to support themselves by doing commercial or semicommercial work for publishers of pictorial material.

Of the 72 plates, Elsholtz signed Nos. 2, 3, 7, 8, 19, 22, 29, 37, 46, 52, 63, 67 and 71; Rechlin signed or initialed Nos. 1, 10, 13, 15, 16, 17, 28, 31, 33, 39, 41, 45, 51, 53, 56 and 72; and Schulz signed Nos. 5, 11, 18, 23, 26, 34, 43, 47, 48, 50, 55, 58, 64, 68 and 70; on the other plates, the signatures are lacking or unclear.

The immediate reason or specific impulse for the publication has not been recorded, but very possibly it was inspired by the mobilization of 1830, when the July Revolution in Paris turned the thoughts of all European rulers to their armies — as a source of protection against their own subjects. The Prussian uniforms and other military trappings so accurately depicted here are representative of the period from about 1815 to 1840 (from the end of the Napoleonic Wars to the end of the reign of Friedrich Wilhelm III); almost yearly some regulation or other would alter a detail or two, but no thoroughgoing change occurred during this timespan.

The basic jacket (with high round collar and short tails) — usually some shade of blue, but green for such infantry groups as the sharpshooters and the jägers (originally huntsmen using their own rifles and long knives), white for cuirassiers, and susceptible of still further variations — was the *Kollett*, not replaced by the typical nineteenth-century *Waffenrock* until the major clothing reform of 1842. It was the same reform that introduced the famous Prussian metal helmet; in these 1830 plates we generally find shakos, busbies or service caps, only the cuirassiers and a few others wearing helmets — which were substantially of leather. (The cuirassiers, who also wore breastplates, were the heavy cavalry. The dragoons were mounted infantry. The hussars — with their characteristic Hungarian-type braided dolmans and fur-trimmed overjackets — were light cavalry used for scouting. The uhlans — a unit inspired by Tatar horsemen — were lancers used for skirmishing.) The trousers in this time period (very modestly depicted in the plates) had flap openings in front; the modern vertical fly was introduced in 1843.

An indispensable reference for those seriously interested in the countless details of nineteenth-century Prussian uniforms and accoutrements — including insignia, footwear, knapsacks, canteens, cartridge pouches, belts, side arms, musical instruments, cockades, fatigue dress and so on — is the copiously illustrated two-volume work by Paul Pietsch, *Die Formations- und Uniformierungs-Geschichte des preussischen Heeres 1804–1914* (2nd edition), Verlag Helmut Gerhard Schulz, Hamburg, 1963 & 1966. A useful source for the history and composition of the various units of the German army (including information on uniforms) is Martin Lezikus' *Die Entwicklung des deutschen Heeres von seinen ersten Anfängen bis auf unsere Tage*, Verlag für Militärgeschichte und Deutsches Schrifttum, Berlin-Fürstenwalde, 1936.

1ᵗᵉˢ Garde Regiment.
(Officier)

bei L.Sachse & Co Berlin.

2

Lith.Inst. v.L.Sachse & Co.

2.tes Garde Regiment
(Tambour.)

3.

Garde Jäger Bataillon.

bei L. Sachse & C⁰ Berlin.

Lith. Inst. v. L. Sachse & C⁰

4.

Garde du Corps.

bei L. Sachse & Co. Berlin.

Lith. Inst. v. L. Sachse & Co.

5.

Garde Husaren Regiment.
(*Rittmeister.*)

6.

1ᵗᵉ Garde Ulanen Regiment.

7.

Kaiser Alexander Grenadier Regiment.
(Fusilier Officier.)

8

Kaiser Franz Grenadier Regiment
(*Unterofficier.*)

9.

Garde Schützen Bataillon.

bei L. Sachse & Co Berlin.

Lith. Inst. v. L. Sachse & Co.

10

Garde Cürassier Regiment.
(*Unterofficier.*)

11.

Garde Dragoner Regiment.
(Trompeter.)

bei L. Sachse & Co. Berlin.

12.

Lith. Inst. v. L. Sachse & Co.

2tes Garde Ulanen Regiment.

13.

1tes Bat. 3ten Garde Landwehr Regiments.

bei L. Sachse & Co. Berlin.

Lith. Inst. v. L. Sachse & Co.

14.

Garde Fuss Artillerie.

bei L. Sachse & Co. Berlin.

Lith. Inst. v. L. Sachse & Co.

15.

Garde Pionier Abtheilung.
(Unterofficier.)

Reitende Garde-Artillerie.

(*Major.*)

bei L. Sachse & Co Berlin.

Lith. Inst. v. L. Sachse & Co.

bei L. Sachse & Cie. Berlin.

Lith. Inst. v. L. Sachse & Co.

17.

Corps Gensd'armerie.
(*Unterofficir.*)

bei L. Sachse & C? Berlin.

Lith. Inst. o. L. Sachse & C?

18.

Garde Unterofficier Compagnie.

19.

1tes Linien Infanterie Regiment.

20

3tes *Linien Infanterie Regiment.*
(Füselier.)

bei L. Sachse u. C.º Berlin.

Lith. Inst. v. L. Sachse u. C.º

21.

4ᵗⁿ Linien Infanterie Regiment
(Hauptmann.)

5.tes Inf: Regiment.   33.tes Inf: Regiment   5.tes Cürassier Regiment.
(Tambour.)

bei L.Sachse & C.º Berlin.

Lith: Inst: v. L. Sachse & Cº.

23.

1es Dragoner Regiment.　　　1e Jäger Abtheilung.

3es Cürassier Regiment.

24.

1tes Husaren Regiment   *1te Pionier Abtheilung.*

1te Artillerie Brigade.

bei L. Sachse & Cie Berlin.

Lith. Inst. v L. Sachse & Cie

COLBERG

9tes Infanterie Regiment.
(Fahnen Unterofficier.)

34tes Infanterie Regiment.
(Unterofficier.)

26.

5tes Husaren Regiment.　　　　　　　2tes Infanterie Regiment.

bei L. Sachse & Co Berlin.　　　　　　Lith. Inst. v. L. Sachse & Co.

27.

21tes Infanterie Regiment.   2tes Cürassier Regiment.

(Trompeter.)

bei L. Sachse & Co. Berlin.

Lith. Inst. v. L. Sachse & Co.

28.

4tes Ulanen Regiment   3tes Dragoner Regiment.
(Officier)

29

2ᵉ Pionier Abtheilung.   *14ᵗᵉˢ Infanterie Regiment.*

bei L. Sachse & Co Berlin.

Lith. Inst. v. L. Sachse & Co.

30

2ᵗᵉ. Artillerie Brigade.   2ᵗᵉ Jäger Abtheilung.

31.

8tes Infanterie Regiment.
(gen. Leib= Regiment.)

bei L. Sachse & Co. Berlin.

Lith. Inst. v. L. Sachse & Co.

bei L. Sachse & Co. Berlin.

Lith. Inst. v. L. Sachse & Co.

32

12tes Jnf: Regiment. 20tes Jnf: Regiment. 24tes Jnf: Regiment.

33.

3te Jäger Abtheilung.
(Officier.)

2tes Dragoner Regiment.
(gen. Prinz Wilhelm.)

34

6.tes Cürassier Regiment.
(gen. Kaiser von Russland.)

3.tes Ulanen Regiment.
(gen. Grossfürst von Russland.)

bei L. Sachse & Co. Berlin.

Lith. Inst. v. L. Sachse & Co.

35.

3tes Husaren Regiment.
(Brandenburgisches.)

3te Pionir Abtheilung.
(Officier und Unterofficier.)

bei L. Sachse & Co. Berlin.

36.

Lith. Inst. v. L. Sachse & Co.

35tes Infanterie Regiment.
(Major.)

3te Artillerie Brigade.
(Rittmeister.)

37.

26stes Infanterie Regiment.   27stes Infanterie Regiment.
(Unterofficier.)

38.

4*te* Pionier Abtheilung.   36*stes* (4*tes* Reserve) Inf. Regt.

(Unterofficier.)

(Interims Uniform.)

39.

31ᵗᵉˢ Infanterie Regiment.   *8ᵗᵉˢ Cürassier Regiment.*

40

12.les Husaren Regiment.　　*32.stes Infanterie Regiment.*

41.

7͟t͟e͟s Cürassier Regiment.
(Wachtmeister.)

10͟t͟e͟s Husaren Regiment.
(Unterofficier.)

42.

4te Jäger Abtheilung.
(Hornist.)

4te Artillerie Brigade.

bei L. Sachse & Co. Berlin.

Lith: Inst: v. L. Sachse & Co.

43.

6tes Infanterie Regiment.   7tes Infanterie Regiment.

44.

18ᵗᵉˢ Infanterie Regiment.　19ᵗᵉˢ Infanterie Regiment.

(Tambour.)　(Tambour Major.)

45.

7tes Husaren Regiment. 37tes (5tes Reserve) Inf. Regiment.

bei L. Sachse & Co. Berlin.

Lith. Inst. v. L. Sachse & Co.

46.

1ste Schützen Abtheilung.   5te Artillerie Brigade.
(Bombardier.)

47.

6tes Ulanen Regiment.
(*Unterofficier*)

1tes Ulanen Regiment.

48.

2tes (gen. 2tes Leib=) Husaren Reg   5te Pionier Abtheilung.
(Officier)   (Hauptmann.)

bei L.Sachse & Co. Berlin.

Lith.Inst. v. L.Sachse & Co.

10tes Infanterie Regiment.
(Hornist.)

11tes Infanterie Regiment.

50.

2ᵗᵉ Schützen Abtheilung.
(Unterofficier.)

22ᵗᵉˢ Infanterie Regiment.

51.

6te Pionier Abtheilung.   38tes (6tes Reserve) Inf. Regiment.

52.

4ᵗᵉˢ Husaren Regiment.
(Trompeter)

6ᵗᵉˢ Husaren Regiment.
(Unterofficier.)

53.

2tes Ulanen Regiment.   6te Artillerie Brigade.
(Unteroffizier.)

54.

1tes Cürassier Regiment.
(Officier.)

23tes Infanterie Regiment.
(Officier.)

55.

16.tes Infanterie Regiment.
(Feldwebel.)

17.tes Infanterie Regiment.
(Hauptmann.)

56.

15tes Infanterie Regiment.   *39tes (7tes Reserve) Infant. Regt.*
(Major.)

bei L. Sachse & Co. Berlin.

Lith. Inst. v. L. Sachse & Co.

3te Schützen Abtheilung.

(Hornist.)

13tes Infanterie Regiment.

(Janitschar.)

58.

8tes Husaren Regiment.
(Unterofficier.)

4tes Cürassier Regiment.
(Standartenträger.)

59.

5tes Ulanen Regiment.   11tes Husaren Regiment.

60.

7te Pionier Abtheilung   *7te Artillerie Brigade.*

(*Unterofficier.*)

bei L. Sachse & Cie. Berlin.

Lith. Inst. v. L. Sachse & Cie.

bei L. Sachse & Co. Berlin.

Lith. Inst. v. L. Sachse & Co.

61.

25ᵗᵉˢ Infanterie Regiment.   29ᵗᵉˢ Infanterie Regiment.
(Major.)

28tes Infanterie Regiment.
(Unterofficier)

9tes Husaren Regiment.

63.

40tes (3tes Reserve) Inf. Regiment. 4te Schützen Abtheilung.

64

30tes Inf. Regiment.
(Fusilier Unterofficier.)

7tes Ulanen Regiment.

bei L. Sachse & C? Berlin.

Lith. Inst. v. L. Sachse & C?

8tes Ulanen-Regiment. *8te Pionier-Abtheilung.*

bei L. Sachse & C? Berlin.

Lith. Inst. v. L. Sachse & C?

8te Artillerie Brigade.   4tes Dragoner Regiment.
(Unterofficier.)

67.

General Staabs Officier.   General.   Adjutant.
(Major)   (Rittmeister)

bei L. Sachse & Co Berlin.   Lith. Inst. von L. Sachse & Co

68.

Auditeur.　　　*Regimentsarzt.*

69.

Cadetten Corps *(zu Berlin.)*

Officier, Cadet.

bei L. Sachse & Co Berlin.

70

Lith. Inst. von L. Sachse & Co.

Reitendes Feldjäger Corps.

71.

Invalide.   *Garnison Compagnie.*   *Landwehrmann.*
(*Unterofficier.*)

79.

20tes Landwehr Cavallerie Regiment.   Landgensd'armerie zu Fass und zu Pferde.
(Unterofficiere)

[THE END]